# Mind Benders® Level 1

## Deductive Thinking Skills

**Mind Benders® Series**
📖 Level 1 📖 Level 2 📖 Verbal 📖 Level 3
📖 Level 4 📖 Level 5 📖 Level 6 📖 Level 7 📖 Level 8

Written by
**Michael Baker**

Graphics by
**Scott Slyter**

© 2005
THE CRITICAL THINKING CO.™
www.CriticalThinking.com
Phone: 800-458-4849 • Fax: 541-756-1758
1991 Sherman Ave., Suite 200 • North Bend • OR 97459
ISBN 978-0-89455-872-6

**Reproduction of This Copyrighted Material**
The intellectual material in this product is the copyrighted property of The Critical Thinking Co.™ The individual or entity who initially purchased this product from The Critical Thinking Co.™ or one of its authorized resellers is licensed to reproduce (print or duplicate on paper) up to 35 copies of each page in this product per year for use within one home or one classroom. Our copyright and this limited reproduction permission (user) agreement strictly prohibit the sale of any of the copyrighted material in this product. Any reproduction beyond these expressed limits is strictly prohibited without the written permission of The Critical Thinking Co.™ Please visit http://www.criticalthinking.com/copyright for more information. The Critical Thinking Co.™ retains full intellectual property rights on all its products (eBooks, books, and software).
Printed in the United States of America by McNaughton & Gunn, Inc., Saline, MI (Jan. 2015)

# TABLE OF CONTENTS

## INTRODUCTORY INFORMATION
    Teaching Suggestions .................................................................................. iii
    How to Use a Chart ..................................................................................... iv

## ACTIVITIES
    Logic .................................................................................... 1-10, 31-34, 43
    Math ........................................................................................ 11-20, 35-38
    Reading ................................................................................... 21-30, 39-42

## SOLUTIONS ............................................................................................ 44

# TEACHING SUGGESTIONS

## PURPOSE

*Mind Benders® Level 1* helps students develop comprehension, deductive reasoning, visual tracking, and fine motor skills. These logic activities can build confidence and improve self-esteem.

## MATERIALS

Use a pencil and have an eraser handy. The clues are challenging; understanding the chart usually takes a little practice.

## BUILDING CONFIDENCE AND IMPROVING SELF-ESTEEM

This type of problem-solving is new to students. Praise students' success with every clue and discuss their determination to finish these challenging activities. My favorite expression to use with students is, "You are so hard-working." Try to instill in them the confidence to apply these problem-solving skills to other schoolwork. Help them to identify themselves as tenacious problem-solvers.

## TEACHING SUGGESTIONS

When you first introduce students to *Mind Benders®*, work through the problems together until the students are confident enough to tackle the problems on their own. As you work through the problems, help them do the following:

1. Understand the chart
   a. Each person, animal, or object in the problem is represented on the chart. When you read the problem to the students, point to each item on the chart. When you read the first couple of clues, point to each item targeted in the clue.
   b. Each person, animal, or object in the chart has its own row or column. The intersection of each row and column is where the students indicate if the relationship is true or false (yes or no is often easier to understand). It may take some practice, but they usually comprehend after completing a few problems.
   c. Teach them to fill in as much information on the chart as they can after each clue. Children commonly begin by trying to solve the *Mind Benders®* without filling in all the "false" (no) relationships. This will work for some of the early problems, but eventually students will encounter more challenging problems. **Ask students to always mark all the true and false (yes and no) information learned from every clue.**

2. Help students understand the clues in the beginning until they have some success and gain some confidence. Then ease off on the help by slowly challenging them to interpret the clues on their own. I frequently tell students that I know they can solve this clue because they have already solved harder clues. Knowing when to help and when to challenge can be difficult, but whether students succeed or become frustrated, praise their effort and their current and/or past success.

3. Pay special attention to the first few problems in each section. It is common for students to perform better in certain sections than in others, so don't be surprised if a student does well in the logic section but struggles in the math section. If a section becomes too frustrating for a student, move to another section. Return to the previous section once the student has had more practice and feels more confident; it is not necessary to go through the book sequentially.

4. In the solutions section, the numbers on each chart indicate the clue(s) used to fill in that square.

5. Have fun! Remember to teach students that critical thinking is fun and compliment their perseverance.

# HOW TO USE A CHART

Each *Mind Benders*® problem gives you a chart and a set of clues. Read the clues very carefully and mark each space true or false (yes or no) in the chart. Many students make the mistake of just marking "true" answers in the chart. This makes the problems harder to solve since "false" answers sometimes lead you to the "true" answer.

## Example: Activity 1

A girl, a boy, and their dad have their own pets. Use the clues and chart to find each one's pet.
1. The boy's pet and the dad's pet have legs.
2. The dad's pet likes to sit on his shoulder.

## Solution:

1. Read clue 1. Look at each of the pets shown at the top of the chart. The bird and the horse have legs, but the snake does not, so the bird and the horse belong to the boy and the dad. If the bird and horse belong to the boy and the dad, the snake must belong to the girl.

2. Mark your answers on the chart. Draw Y for yes in the box under the snake in the girl's row. Draw N for no in the other two boxes under the snake and in the other two boxes in the girl's row. Look at your chart; it shows the snake belongs to the girl, not to the boy or the dad.

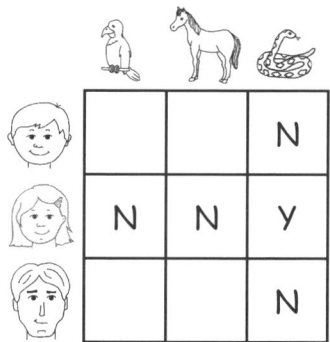

3. Read clue 2. Could a bird sit on the dad's shoulder? Could a horse sit on the dad's shoulder? This clue tells us that the dad's pet is the bird.

4. Mark your answers on the chart. Draw Y for yes in the box under the bird in the dad's row. Draw N for no in the other empty box under the bird and in the other empty box in the dad's row. This means that the bird belongs to the dad, not to the boy.

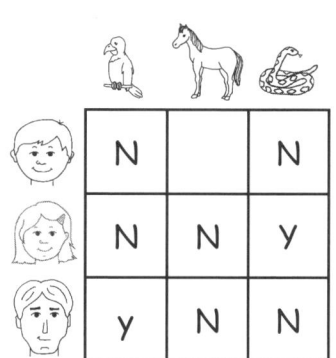

5. Look at the chart. If the snake belongs to the girl and the bird belongs to the dad, then the horse must belong to the boy. Draw Y for yes in the last empty box.

# ACTIVITY 1

Directions: Fill in the chart using Y for yes or N for no as you solve the puzzle.

A girl, a boy, and a dog all live in different houses. Use the clues and the chart to find each one's home.

1. The boy's house is the widest.
2. The dog's house is not the smallest.

Mind Benders® Level 1     Activities – Logic

# ACTIVITY 2

Directions: Fill in the chart using Y for yes or N for no as you solve the puzzle.

A boy, a girl, and their dad all have their own pets. Use the clues and the chart to find each one's pet.

1. The dad found his pet crying in a tree.
2. The boy's pet sleeps in the boy's bed every night.

Mind Benders® Level 1                                      Activities – Logic

# ACTIVITY 3

Directions: Fill in the chart using Y for yes or N for no as you solve the puzzle.

A girl, boy, and rabbit all live in different houses. Use the clue and the chart to find each one's house.

1. The one with the longest hair lives in the biggest house.

Mind Benders® Level 1                                    Activities – Logic

# ACTIVITY 4

Directions: Fill in the chart using Y for yes or N for no as you solve the puzzle.

A father, his daughter, and his son will each wear a different shirt today. Use the clues and the chart to find each one's shirt.

1. The father will not wear stripes.
2. The daughter will not wear anything black or striped.

# ACTIVITY 5

Directions: Fill in the chart using Y for yes or N for no as you solve the puzzle.

A boy, a girl, and their dad each has a pet dog. Use the clues and the chart to find each one's pet.

1. The girl's dog wears a collar and is smaller than her dad's dog.
2. The dad's dog is not the biggest or the smallest.

Mind Benders® Level 1        Activities – Logic

# ACTIVITY 6

Directions: Fill in the chart using Y for yes or N for no as you solve the puzzle.

A boy, a girl, and their mom have different pet fish. Use the clues and the chart to find who owns each fish.

1. The mother and daughter have smaller fish.
2. The tallest owner has the smallest fish.

# ACTIVITY 7

Directions: Fill in the chart using Y for yes or N for no as you solve the puzzle.

A girl, a boy, and their mom all have different bowls of food. Use the clues and the chart to find each one's bowl.

1. The mother's bowl is not the smallest.
2. Everyone is waiting for the girl's food to cool off since it is the hottest.

# ACTIVITY 8

Directions: Fill in the chart using Y for yes or N for no as you solve the puzzle.

A girl, a boy, and a dog all have favorite bowls. Use the clues and the chart to find each one's favorite bowl.

1. The dog's bowl will fit in the girl's bowl.
2. The boy's bowl is smaller than the dog's bowl.

Mind Benders® Level 1    Activities – Logic

# ACTIVITY 9

**Directions:** Fill in the chart using Y for yes or N for no as you solve the puzzle.

A boy, a girl, and their grandmother all fly different airplanes. Use the clues and the chart to find each one's airplane.

1. Grandma's plane is not the smallest or the largest.
2. The boy was older than the girl last year.
3. The youngest person's plane is not the smallest.

Mind Benders® Level 1                                  Activities – Logic

# ACTIVITY 10

Directions: Fill in the chart using Y for yes or N for no as you solve the puzzle.

A girl, a boy, and their mother all drank some water. Use the clues and the chart to find each one's glass.

1. The mom's glass and the girl's glass are less full.
2. The mom's glass and the boy's glass are more full.

Mind Benders® Level 1　　　　　　　　　　　　　　　　Activities – Math

# ACTIVITY 11

Directions: Fill in the chart using Y for yes or N for no as you solve the puzzle.

A girl, a boy, and a cat all live in different houses. Use the clues and the chart to find each one's house.

1. The cat's house has the fewest windows.
2. The girl's house has one more window than the cat's house.

Mind Benders® Level 1            Activities – Math

# ACTIVITY 12

Directions: Fill in the chart using Y for yes or N for no as you solve the puzzle.

A girl, a boy, and a cat all have birthdays today. Use the clues and the chart to find each one's age.

1. The cat was the youngest last year.
2. The boy is not the oldest.

Mind Benders® Level 1                                     Activities – Math

# ACTIVITY 13

**Directions:** Fill in the chart using Y for yes or N for no as you solve the puzzle.

A cat, a boy, and a girl are all different ages.
Use the clues and the chart to find each one's age.

1. The eight-year-old does not have a tail.
2. The boy is not the oldest or the youngest.

Mind Benders® Level 1                Activities – Math

# ACTIVITY 14

Directions: Fill in the chart using Y for yes or N for no as you solve the puzzle.

An alligator, a boy, and a girl are all different ages. Use the clues and the chart to find each one's age.

1. The alligator is no longer four.
2. The boy was four two years ago.

# ACTIVITY 15

Directions: Fill in the chart using Y for yes or N for no as you solve the puzzle.

A duck, an owl, and a squirrel are all different ages. Use the clues and the chart to find each one's age.

1. The animal without feathers was five last year.
2. The oldest animal spends a lot of time in the water.

Mind Benders® Level 1  Activities – Math

# ACTIVITY 16

Directions: Fill in the chart using Y for yes or N for no as you solve the puzzle.

A boy, a turtle, and a girl are all different ages. Use the clues and the chart to find each one's age.

1. The turtle is twice as old as the youngest.
2. The turtle is two years younger than Tina.

Mind Benders® Level 1     Activities – Math

# ACTIVITY 17

Directions: Fill in the chart using Y for yes or N for no as you solve the puzzle.

A boy, a duck, and a horse are all different ages. Use the clues and the chart to find each one's age.

1. The one without the tail is three years younger than the oldest.
2. The duck will be six next year.

Mind Benders® Level 1                                          Activities – Math

# ACTIVITY 18

Directions: Fill in the chart using Y for yes or N for no as you solve the puzzle.

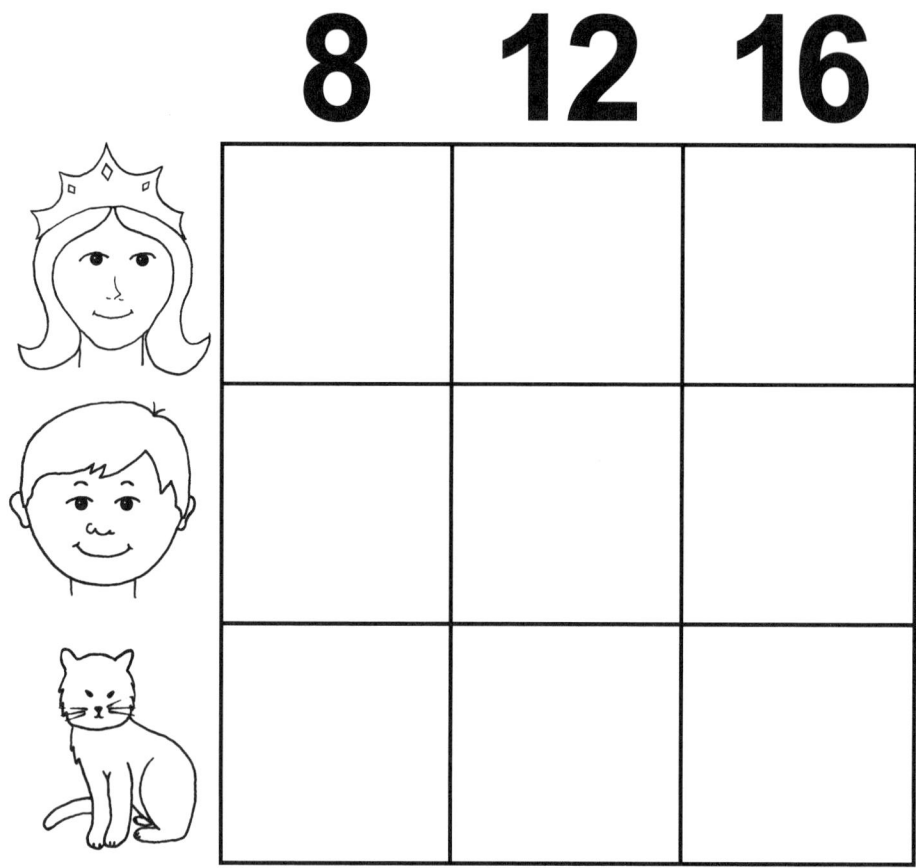

A princess, a boy, and a cat are all different ages. Use the clues and the chart to find each one's age.

1. The boy was playing with the cat the day the princess was born.
2. The cat was lonely until the boy was born.

# ACTIVITY 19

Directions: Fill in the chart using Y for yes or N for no as you solve the puzzle.

A girl, a duck, and a cat are all different ages. Use the clues and the chart to find each one's age.

1. The one without hair will be nine on her birthday.
2. The one who reads is twice as old as the youngest.

Mind Benders® Level 1                                        Activities – Math

# ACTIVITY 20

Directions: Fill in the chart using Y for yes or N for no as you solve the puzzle.

A boy, a girl, and a shark all are different ages. Use the clues and the chart to find each one's age.

1. Seven years ago, the shark had not been born.
2. The girl has had three more birthdays than the boy.

Mind Benders® Level 1                                                Activities – Reading

# ACTIVITY 21

Directions: Fill in the chart using Y for yes or N for no as you solve the puzzle.

A boy, a girl, and their dad each has a favorite pet. Use the clues and the chart to find each one's pet.

1. The dad's pet has paws, but it does not bark.
2. The girl's pet does not bark.

Mind Benders® Level 1 Activities – Reading

# ACTIVITY 22

Directions: Fill in the chart using Y for yes or N for no as you solve the puzzle.

A boy, a girl, and a worm each has a favorite fruit. Use the clues and the chart to find each one's fruit.

1. The girl's favorite fruit begins with an "a."
2. The worm does not like the fruit that rhymes with "bear."

# ACTIVITY 23

Directions: Fill in the chart using Y for yes or N for no as you solve the puzzle.

A girl, a boy, and their mom each has a favorite sport. Use the clues and the chart to find their sports.

1. The mom's sport does not use a bat to hit the ball.
2. The boy's sport uses the biggest ball.

# ACTIVITY 24

Directions: Fill in the chart using Y for yes or N for no as you solve the puzzle.

A boy, a girl, and a teacher all get to school a different way. Use the clues and the chart to find how each one gets to school.

1. The boy wishes he could ride to school in a truck.
2. The girl sits in the sixth row of seats.

Mind Benders® Level 1   Activities – Reading

# ACTIVITY 25

**Directions:** Fill in the chart using Y for yes or N for no as you solve the puzzle.

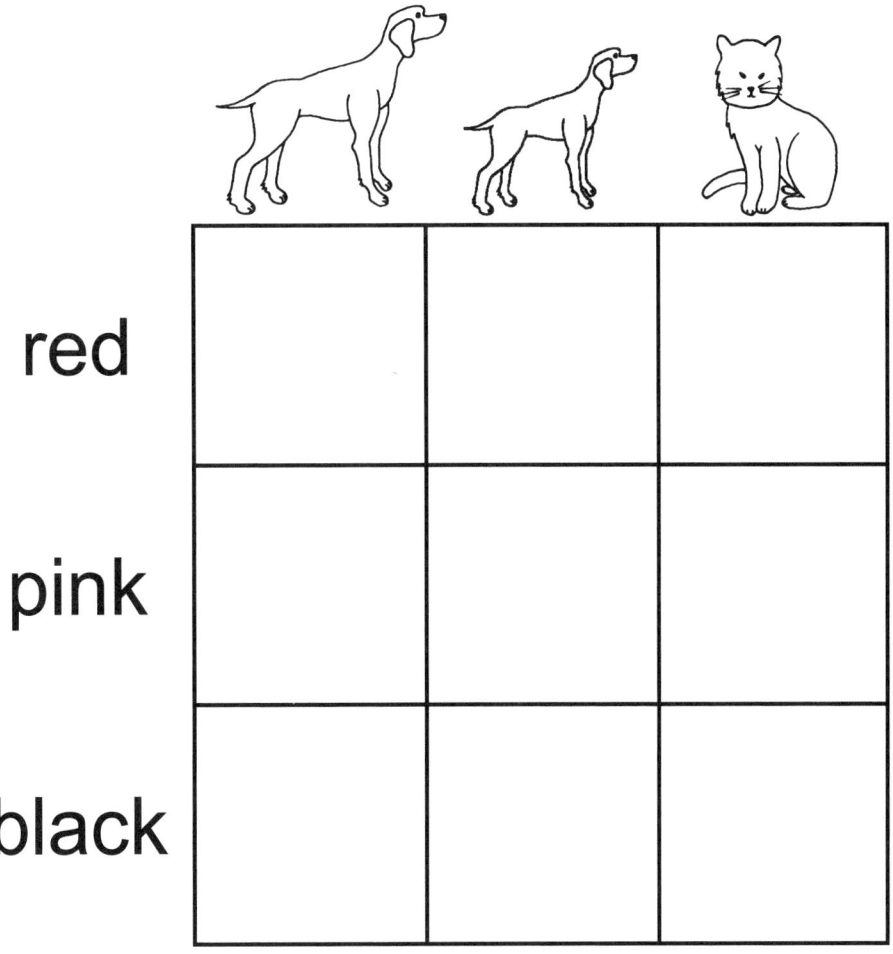

A big dog, a small dog, and a cat each has a favorite color. Use the clues and the chart to find each one's favorite color.

1. The big dog and the cat like colors that end in "k."
2. The big dog likes the darkest color.

# ACTIVITY 26

Directions: Fill in the chart using Y for yes or N for no as you solve the puzzle.

A dinosaur, a shark, and a girl all have different names. Use the clues and the chart to find each one's name.

1. The one whose name rhymes with "ham" does not have a tail.
2. Tim is a better swimmer than Bill.

# ACTIVITY 27

**Directions:** Fill in the chart using Y for yes or N for no as you solve the puzzle.

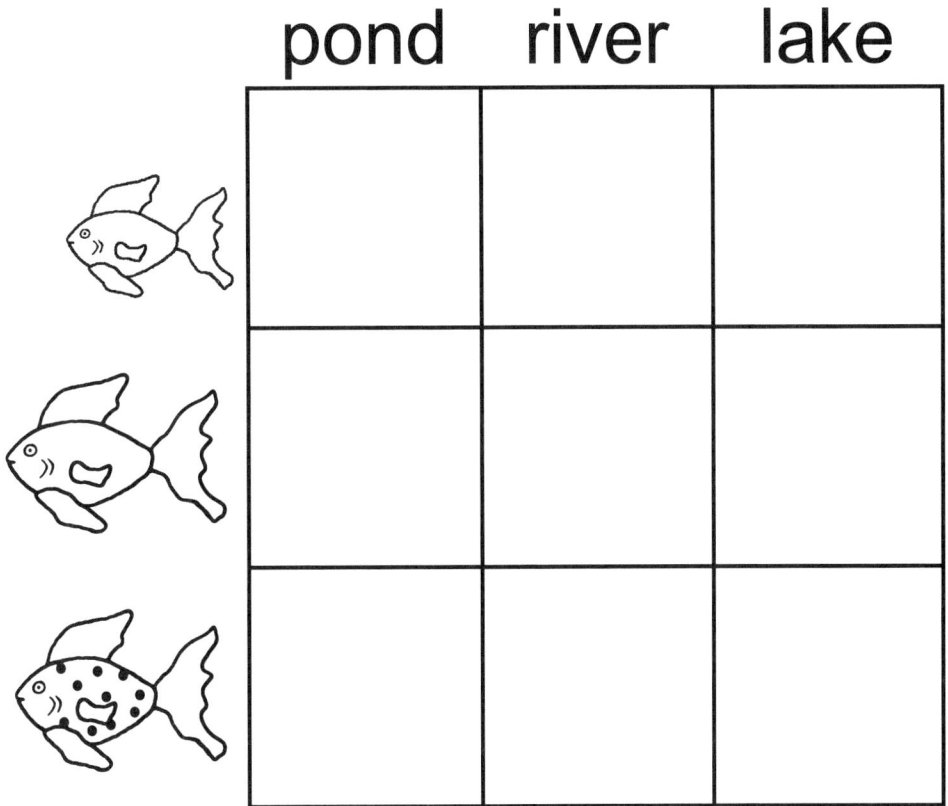

None of these fish lives in the same place. Use the clues and the chart to find their homes.

1. The smallest fish has the longest home.
2. The spotted fish's home is not the smallest.

Mind Benders® Level 1    Activities – Reading

# ACTIVITY 28

Directions: Fill in the chart using Y for yes or N for no as you solve the puzzle.

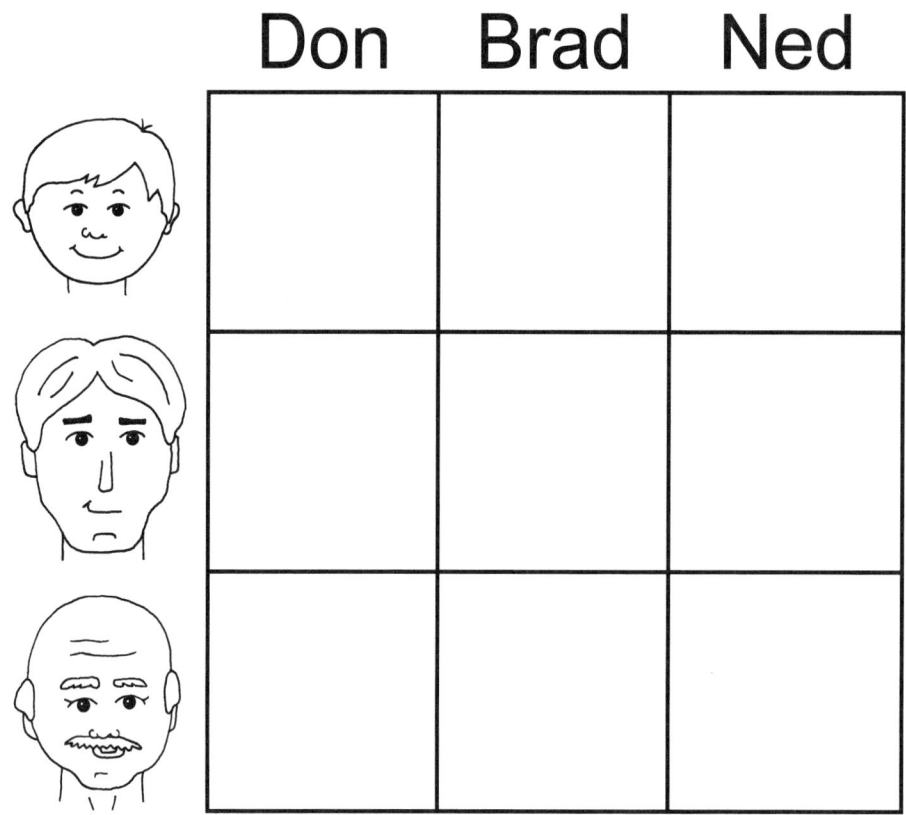

A boy, his dad, and his grandfather all have different names. Use the clues and the chart to find each one's name.

1. The boy's name does not rhyme with "red."
2. The dad's name begins with the same letter sound as "barn."

Mind Benders® Level 1                                   Activities – Reading

# ACTIVITY 29

Directions: Fill in the chart using Y for yes or N for no as you solve the puzzle.

A girl, a boy, and their grandfather all have their own pets. Use the clues and the chart to find each one's pet.

1. The girl's pet rhymes with "rat," but cannot fly.
2. The grandfather's pet rhymes with "wish."

Mind Benders® Level 1     Activities – Reading

# ACTIVITY 30

Directions: Fill in the chart using Y for yes or N for no as you solve the puzzle.

A cat, a dog, and a pig each saw something in the sky. Use the clues and the chart to find out what each one saw.

1. The cat and the pig saw things that flew away from them.
2. The pig did not see something with feathers.

Mind Benders® Level 1 — Activities – Logic

# ACTIVITY 31

Directions: Fill in the chart using Y for yes or N for no as you solve the puzzle.

A girl, a boy, a dad, and a mom all have different cats. Use the clues and the chart to find each one's cat.

1. The girl's cat is not the smallest and does not have a dark tail.

2. The dad's cat is not the biggest and does not have a dark tail.

3. On the chart, the mom's cat is closer to the dad's cat than the boy's cat.

Mind Benders® Level 1　　　　　　　　　　　　　　　　　　Activities – Logic

# ACTIVITY 32

Directions: Fill in the chart using Y for yes or N for no as you solve the puzzle.

A boy, a girl, a teacher, and a dog all live in different homes. Use the clues and the chart to find each one's home.

1. The teacher's house has two windows and is next to the girl's house.
2. The girl's house is on one end of the chart and does not have two windows.
3. The boy's house has a pointed roof.

Mind Benders® Level 1 — Activities – Logic

# ACTIVITY 33

**Directions:** Fill in the chart using Y for yes or N for no as you solve the puzzle.

A girl, a boy, a cat, and a dog all have different bowls. Use the clues and the chart to find each one's bowl.

1. The dog and cat are never served hot food.
2. The boy's bowl is not hot.
3. The dog's bowl has the most food in it and is the same size as the cat's bowl.

Mind Benders® Level 1  Activities – Logic

# ACTIVITY 34

**Directions:** Fill in the chart using Y for yes or N for no as you solve the puzzle.

A girl, a boy, a mom, and a dad all own different fish. Use the clues and the chart to find each one's fish.

1. The mom's fish is bigger than the dad's fish and the girl's fish.
2. The boy's fish is bigger than the mom's fish.
3. The dad's fish is not the smallest.

# ACTIVITY 35

**Directions:** Fill in the chart using Y for yes or N for no as you solve the puzzle.

|   | 1 | 3 | 4 | 6 |
|---|---|---|---|---|
| daughter |  |  |  |  |
| son |  |  |  |  |
| mother |  |  |  |  |
| father |  |  |  |  |

The Smith family went fishing. Everyone caught fish. Use the clues and the chart to find out how many fish each person caught.

1. Mr. and Mrs. Smith did not catch the fewest or the most fish.
2. The daughter caught fewer fish than her brother.
3. The mother caught more fish than the father.

Mind Benders® Level 1                                  Activities – Math

# ACTIVITY 36

Directions: Fill in the chart using Y for yes or N for no as you solve the puzzle.

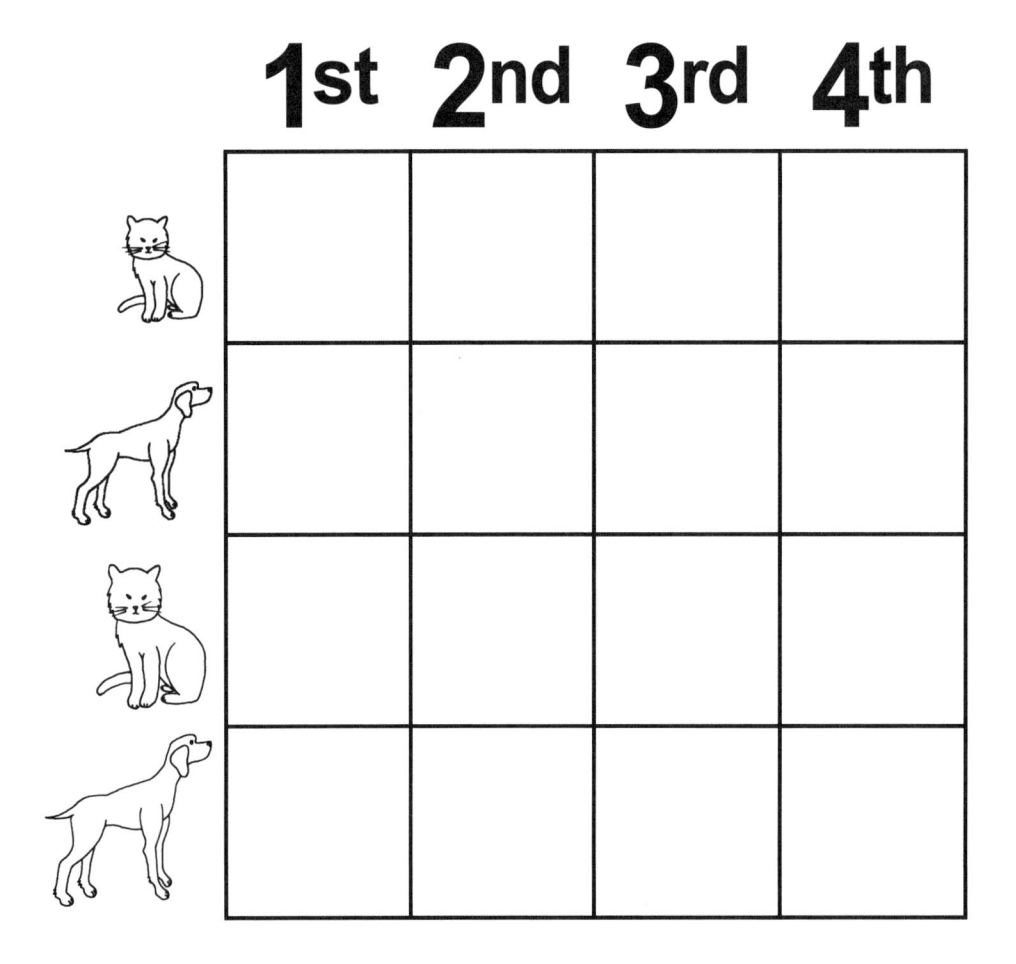

**1st  2nd  3rd  4th**

|     | 1st | 2nd | 3rd | 4th |
|-----|-----|-----|-----|-----|
| 🐱 small cat |  |  |  |  |
| 🐕 big dog |  |  |  |  |
| 🐱 big cat |  |  |  |  |
| 🐕 small dog |  |  |  |  |

A small cat, a small dog, a big cat, and a big dog had a running race. Use the clues and the chart to see how they placed.

1. A cat was first and third.
2. The little dog finished before the little cat and the big dog.

36                      © 2005 The Critical Thinking Co.™ • www.CriticalThinking.com • 800-458-4849

Mind Benders® Level 1　　　　　　　　　　　　　　　　Activities – Math

# ACTIVITY 37

**Directions:** Fill in the chart using Y for yes or N for no as you solve the puzzle.

**6　7　8　9**

A shark, a cat, a dog, and a duck are all different ages. Use the clues and the chart to find each one's age.

1. The animals whose total number of legs adds up to eight are not the oldest or youngest.
2. The oldest does not have any fins.
3. One year ago, the dog was at the cat's 7th birthday party.

© 2005 The Critical Thinking Co.™ • www.CriticalThinking.com • 800-458-4849　　37

## ACTIVITY 38

**Directions:** Fill in the chart using Y for yes or N for no as you solve the puzzle.

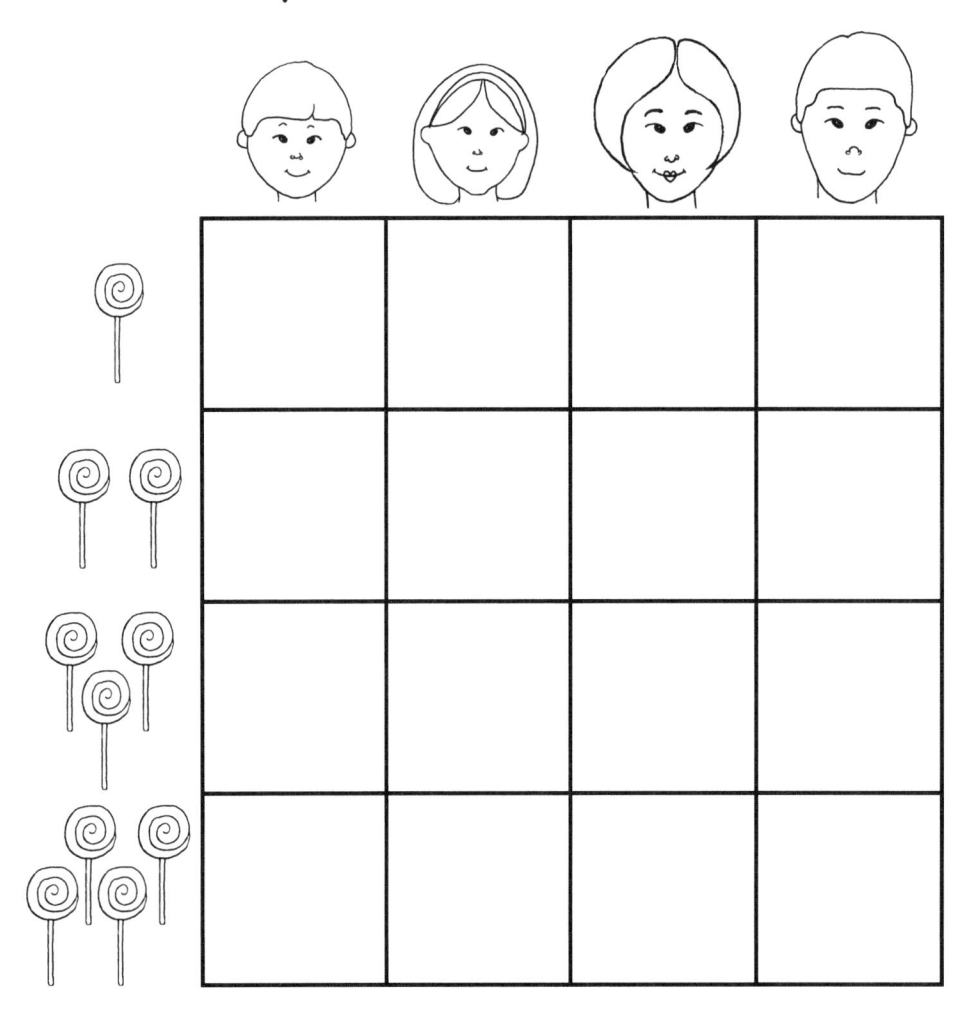

A boy, a girl, a mother, and a father each bought suckers at the store. Use the clues and the chart to find out how many suckers each person bought.

1. The boy bought two more suckers than his mom, who had the fewest.

2. The father bought more than one sucker, but fewer suckers than the boy bought.

Mind Benders® Level 1    Activities – Reading

# ACTIVITY 39

**Directions:** Fill in the chart using Y for yes or N for no as you solve the puzzle.

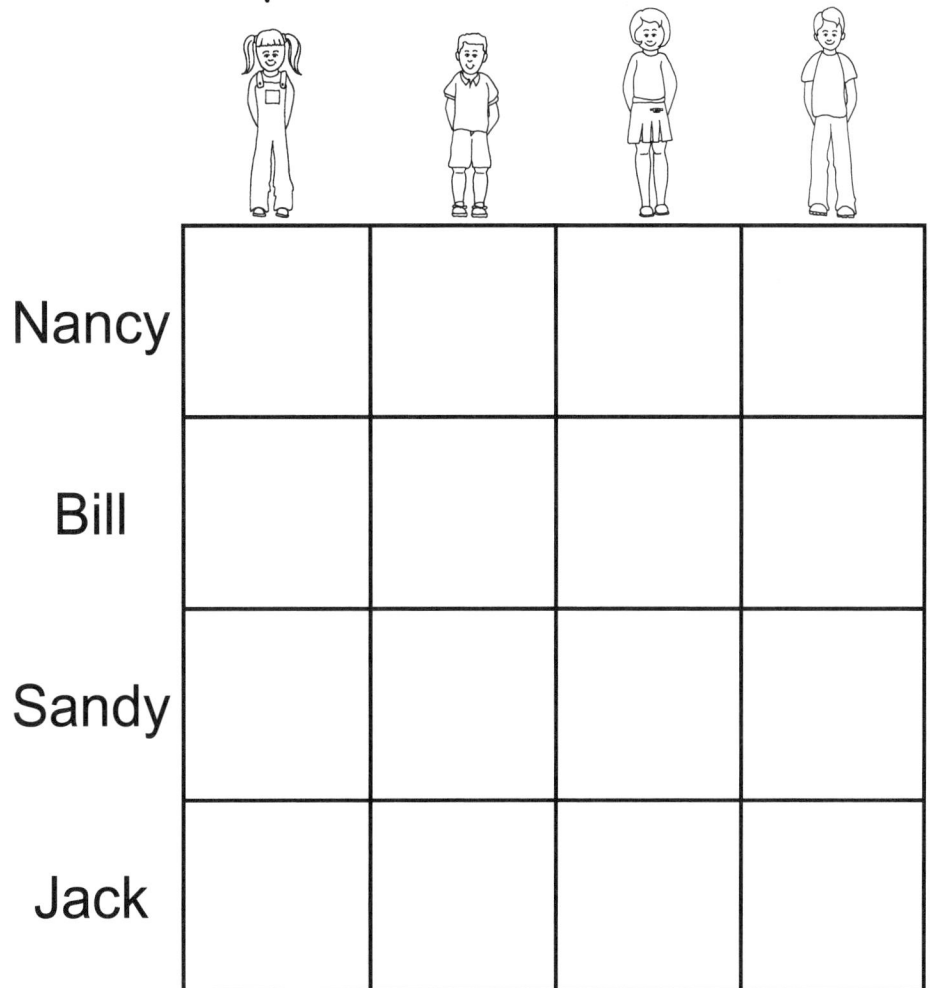

|        | | | | |
|--------|---|---|---|---|
| Nancy  | | | | |
| Bill   | | | | |
| Sandy  | | | | |
| Jack   | | | | |

Nancy, Bill, Sandy, and Jack are all members of the same family. Use the clue and the chart to find out who has which name.

1. Bill is taller than Jack and Nancy.

© 2005 The Critical Thinking Co.™ • www.CriticalThinking.com • 800-458-4849

Mind Benders® Level 1          Activities – Reading

# ACTIVITY 40

**Directions:** Fill in the chart using Y for yes or N for no as you solve the puzzle.

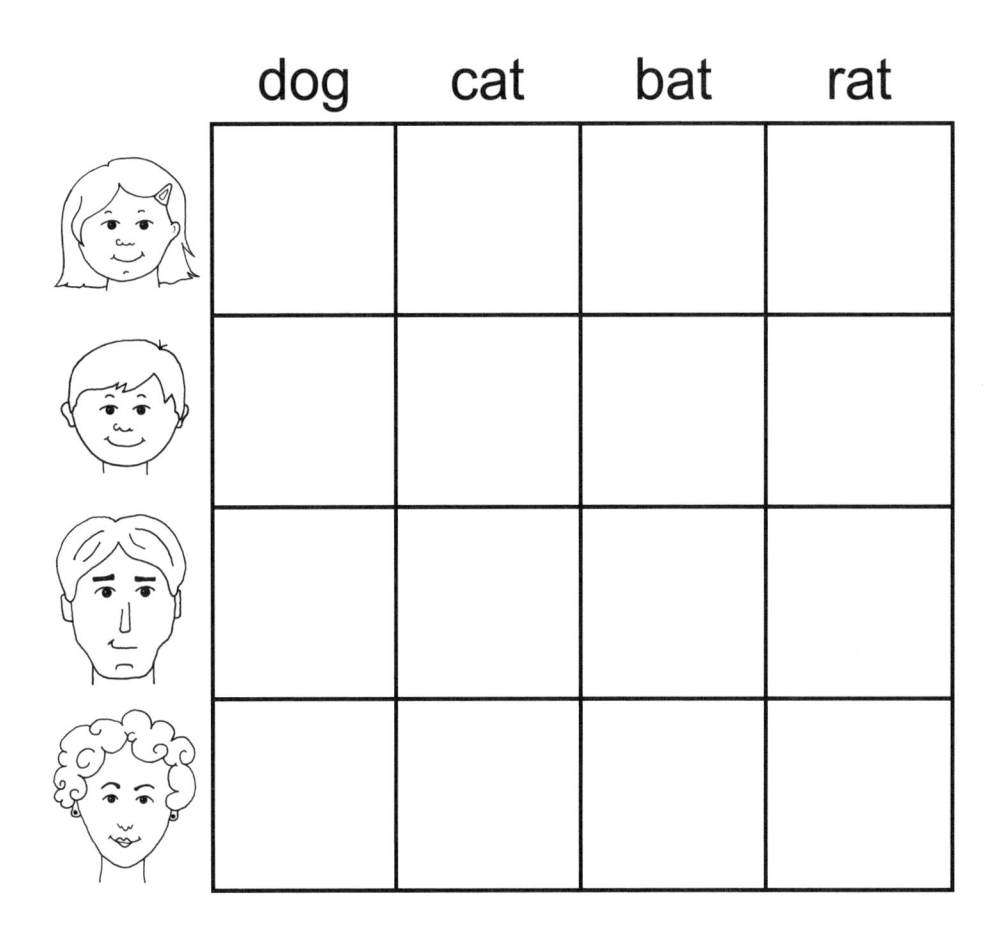

|  | dog | cat | bat | rat |
|---|---|---|---|---|
| girl |  |  |  |  |
| boy |  |  |  |  |
| dad |  |  |  |  |
| mom |  |  |  |  |

A girl, a boy, a dad, and a mom all have different pets. Use the clues and the chart to find each one's pet.

1. The name of the dad's pet does not rhyme with any of the other pet names.

2. The name of the girl's pet rhymes with "rat" and with the name of the mom's pet.

3. The name of the mom's pet rhymes with "cat."

# ACTIVITY 41

Directions: Fill in the chart using Y for yes or N for no as you solve the puzzle.

|  |  |  |  |  |
|---|---|---|---|---|
| Sue |  |  |  |  |
| Tom |  |  |  |  |
| Mike |  |  |  |  |
| Linda |  |  |  |  |

Sue, Tom, Mike, and Linda are all members of the same family. Use the clue and the chart to find out who has which name.

1. Tom is taller than Linda.

Mind Benders® Level 1  Activities – Reading

# ACTIVITY 42

Directions: Fill in the chart using Y for yes or N for no as you solve the puzzle.

A girl, a boy, a man, and a woman all took trips to visit family relatives. Use the clues and the chart to find out how each person traveled.

1. The woman's hair was rained on throughout her trip.

2. The boy got to look out sixteen different windows.

3. The girl put her purse next to her and her suitcase in the trunk.

## ACTIVITY 43

**Directions:** Fill in the chart using Y for yes or N for no as you solve the puzzle.

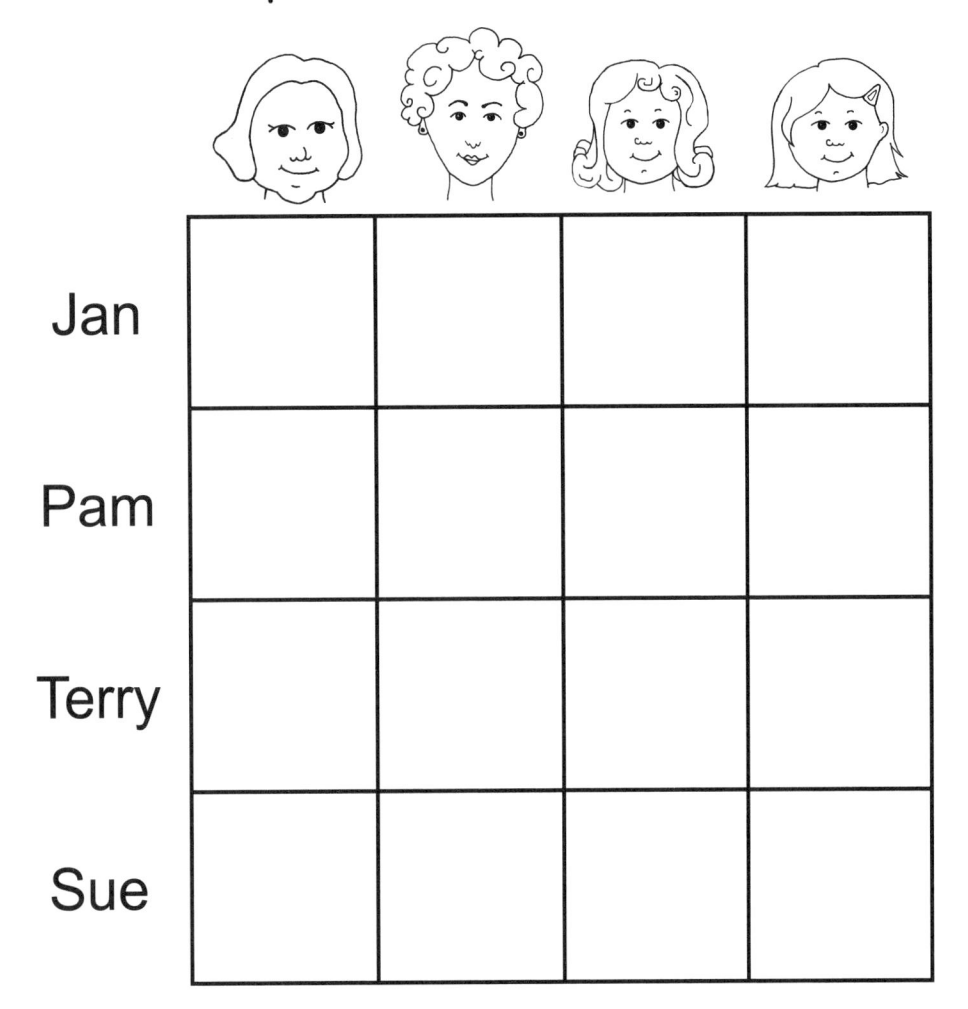

|  | | | | |
|---|---|---|---|---|
| Jan | | | | |
| Pam | | | | |
| Terry | | | | |
| Sue | | | | |

Jan, Pam, Terry, and Sue are all members of the same family. Use the clues and the chart to find out who has which name.

1. Jan drives Pam and Terry to play in their girls' soccer game.
2. Sue used to drive Jan to school.
3. Pam likes Terry's straight hair.

Mind Benders® Level 1 — Solutions

## Page 1

|   | Y₂ | N₁ | N₂ |
|---|---|---|---|
|   | N₁ | Y₁ | N₁ |
|   | N₂ | N₁ | Y₂ |

Clue 1 states that the boy lives in the widest house, which is the house in the middle. Clue 2 states that the dog's house is not the smallest. So the dog lives in the biggest house and the girl lives in the smallest house.

## Page 2

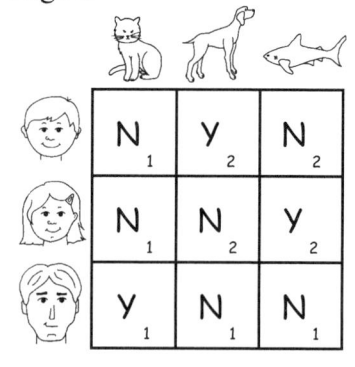

|   | N₁ | Y₂ | N₂ |
|---|---|---|---|
|   | N₁ | N₂ | Y₂ |
|   | Y₁ | N₁ | N₁ |

Clue 1 states that the dad's pet was crying in a tree. Only the cat could climb a tree, so the dad's pet is the cat. Clue 2 states that the boy's pet sleeps in his bed. A shark cannot sleep in a bed, so the boy's pet is the dog. That means that the girl's pet is the shark.

## Page 3

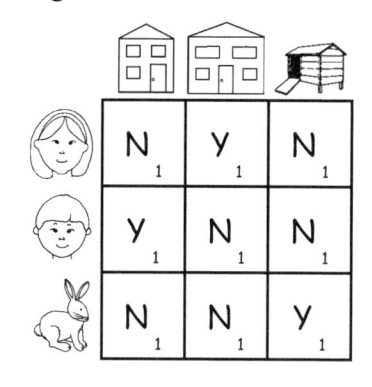

|   | N₁ | Y₁ | N₁ |
|---|---|---|---|
|   | Y₁ | N₁ | N₁ |
|   | N₁ | N₁ | Y₁ |

Clue 1 states that the one with the longest hair lives in the biggest house. The little girl has the longest hair, so she lives in the house in the middle, which is the biggest. Since one of the houses is a rabbit hutch, the rabbit must live in that. Then the boy lives in the other house.

## Page 4

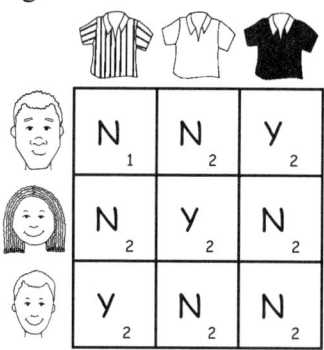

|   | N₁ | N₂ | Y₂ |
|---|---|---|---|
|   | N₂ | Y₂ | N₂ |
|   | Y₂ | N₂ | N₂ |

Clue 1 states that the father will not wear stripes, so the father will wear either the black shirt or the white shirt. Clue 2 states that the daughter will not wear anything black or striped. That leaves the white shirt, so the daughter will wear the white shirt. Then the father will wear the black shirt and the son will wear the striped shirt.

## Page 5

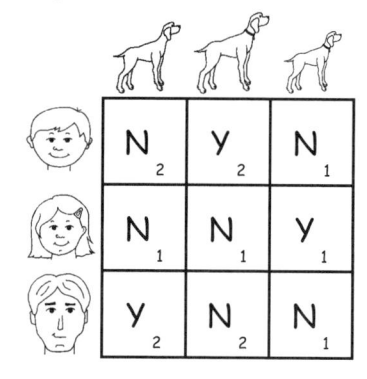

|   | N₂ | Y₂ | N₁ |
|---|---|---|---|
|   | N₁ | N₁ | Y₁ |
|   | Y₂ | N₂ | N₁ |

Based on Clue 1, the girl's dog is the smallest dog on the right since the other dog with a collar is big. Clue 2 states that the dad's dog is not the biggest or smallest, so it is the middle-sized dog on the left. That means the boy's dog is the biggest dog.

## Page 6

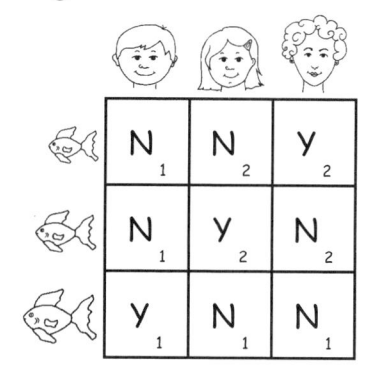

|   | N₁ | N₂ | Y₂ |
|---|---|---|---|
|   | N₁ | Y₂ | N₂ |
|   | Y₁ | N₁ | N₁ |

Based on Clue 1, the boy has the biggest fish. Clue 2 says that the tallest owner has the smallest fish. Since the mother is the tallest, she has the smallest fish. So the girl has the middle-sized fish.

Mind Benders® Level 1 — Solutions

## Page 7

|        | (ice cream) | (noodles hot) | (noodles) |
|--------|---|---|---|
| girl   | N₂ | Y₂ | N₂ |
| boy    | Y₂ | N₂ | N₂ |
| mother | N₁ | N₂ | Y₂ |

Based on Clue 1, the mother has one of the two bowls of noodles since the ice cream is the smallest. Clue 2 states that the girl has the hottest food, so she has the bowl in the middle with the steam. Then the mother has the bowl on the right, and the boy has the ice cream.

## Page 8

|       | med | large | small |
|-------|---|---|---|
| girl  | N₂ | Y₂ | N₂ |
| boy   | N₂ | N₂ | Y₂ |
| dog   | Y₂ | N₁ | N₂ |

Based on Clue 1, the dog's bowl will fit in the girl's bowl, which means it's either the medium or small bowl, not the large bowl. Clue 2 says that the boy's bowl is smaller than the dog's, so the boy's bowl is the small one, and the dog's is the medium bowl, leaving the large bowl as the girl's.

## Page 9

|             | plane1 | plane2 | plane3 |
|-------------|---|---|---|
| boy         | Y₃,₂ | N₁ | N₃,₂ |
| girl        | N₃,₂ | N₁ | Y₃,₂ |
| grandmother | N₁ | Y₁ | N₁ |

Clue 1 tells you that the grandmother's plane is not the smallest or largest, so grandmother's plane is the middle-sized plane in the middle column. Then the boy and the girl have the largest and smallest planes. Clue 2 states that the boy is older than the girl. Use this information with Clue 3 to conclude that since the girl is the youngest, her plane is the largest, and the boy's plane is the smallest.

## Page 10

|      | glass1 | glass2 | glass3 |
|------|---|---|---|
| girl | N₁ | N₂ | Y₂ |
| boy  | Y₁ | N₁ | N₁ |
| mom  | N₁ | Y₂ | N₂ |

Based on Clue 1, the mom's and the girl's glasses are less full, so neither has the fullest glass, which must be the boy's. Clue 2 says that mom's and the boy's glasses both are fuller, so the mom's has to be the medium glass. That leaves the least full glass as the girl's.

## Page 11

|      | house1 | house2 | house3 |
|------|---|---|---|
| girl | N₁ | Y₂ | N₂ |
| boy  | N₁ | N₂ | Y₂ |
| cat  | Y₁ | N₁ | N₁ |

Clue 1 states that the cat's house has the fewest windows, so it's the three-window house. Clue 2 says that the girl's house has one more window than the cat's, so it's the four-window house. That leaves the five-window house as the boy's.

## Page 12

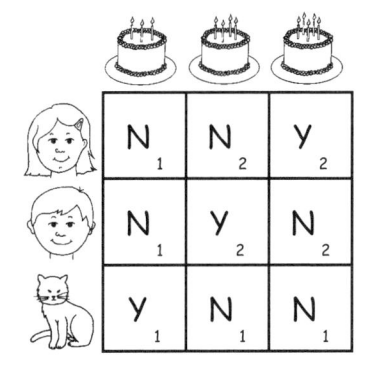

|      | cake1 | cake2 | cake3 |
|------|---|---|---|
| girl | N₁ | N₂ | Y₂ |
| boy  | N₁ | Y₂ | N₂ |
| cat  | Y₁ | N₁ | N₁ |

Clue 1 says that the cat was the youngest, whether last year or any year. So the cat is three years old and has the cake with three candles on it. The boy and the girl are both older than the cat. Clue 2 states that the boy is not the oldest, so he is not five. Since the cat is three, the boy must be four. The girl is the oldest at five.

Mind Benders® Level 1 — Solutions

## Page 13

|  | 3 | 6 | 8 |
|---|---|---|---|
| cat | Y₂ | N₂ | N₁ |
| boy | N₂ | Y₂ | N₂ |
| girl | N₂ | N₂ | Y₂ |

Clue 1 states that the eight-year-old has no tail. The cat has a tail, so it can't be eight, but it could be three or six. Either the girl or the boy could be eight since they have no tails. Clue 2 states that the boy is not the oldest or the youngest, so he's not eight or three. That means the boy is six, so the cat is three, and the girl is eight.

## Page 14

|  | 4 | 5 | 6 |
|---|---|---|---|
| alligator | N₁ | Y₂ | N₂ |
| boy | N₂ | N₂ | Y₂ |
| girl | Y₂ | N₂ | N₂ |

Clue 1, which says that the alligator is no longer four, means it was four at one time, so now must be either five or six. Clue 2 says that the boy was four two years ago, which makes him six now. The alligator is five and that makes the girl the only age left: four.

## Page 15

|  | 5 | 6 | 10 |
|---|---|---|---|
| duck | N₂ | N₁ | Y₂ |
| owl | Y₂ | N₁ | N₂ |
| squirrel | N₁ | Y₁ | N₁ |

Using Clue 1, the only animal without feathers is the squirrel. If the squirrel was five last year, then it's six now. Clue 2 says that the oldest, which would be ten, spends a lot of time in the water. Since the owl doesn't spend time in the water, then the duck has to be ten. That means the owl is five.

## Page 16

|  | 3 | 6 | 8 |
|---|---|---|---|
| boy | Y₂ | N₁ | N₂ |
| turtle | N₁ | Y₁ | N₁ |
| girl | N₂ | N₁ | Y₂ |

Clue 1 says that the turtle is two times as old as the youngest. The youngest is three, so the turtle is six. Clue 2 states that the turtle is two years younger than Tina. Tina is a girl's name, and she's two years older than the turtle, which makes her eight. That means that the boy is the youngest at three.

## Page 17

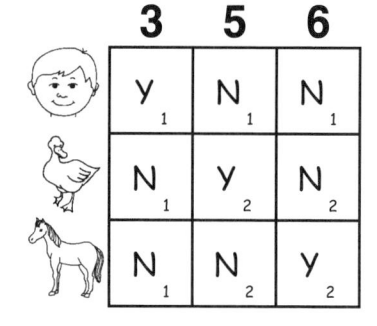

|  | 3 | 5 | 6 |
|---|---|---|---|
| boy | Y₁ | N₁ | N₁ |
| duck | N₁ | Y₂ | N₂ |
| horse | N₁ | N₂ | Y₂ |

Clue 1 states that the one without the tail is three years younger than the oldest. First, the boy is the only one without a tail. Second, the oldest is six and three years younger than that equals three. So the boy is three. Clue 2 states that the duck will be six next year, so it is five this year. That means that the horse must be six.

## Page 18

|  | 8 | 12 | 16 |
|---|---|---|---|
| princess | Y₁ | N₁ | N₁ |
| boy | N₁ | Y₂ | N₂ |
| cat | N₁ | N₂ | Y₂ |

Based on Clue 1, both the boy and the cat are older than the princess since they were both alive when she was born. That means the princess is the youngest at eight. Clue 2 says that the cat was lonely before the boy was born, so the cat is older than the boy. The cat is sixteen, and the boy is twelve.

# Mind Benders® Level 1 — Solutions

## Page 19

|  | 5 | 8 | 10 |
|---|---|---|---|
| girl | N₂ | N₁ | Y₂ |
| duck | N₁ | Y₁ | N₁ |
| cat | Y₂ | N₁ | N₂ |

Clue 1 states that the one without hair will be nine, which means it is eight now. Since the cat and the girl have hair, that means the duck, which has feathers, is eight. Clue 2 says that the one who reads, and only the girl can read, is twice as old as the youngest. Two times five, the youngest, equals ten. So the girl is ten, and the cat is five.

## Page 20

|  | 6 | 8 | 11 |
|---|---|---|---|
| boy | N₁ | Y₂ | N₂ |
| shark | Y₁ | N₁ | N₁ |
| girl | N₁ | N₂ | Y₂ |

Clue 1 states that seven years ago the shark had not been born. So the shark must be six. Clue 2 states that the girl is three years older than the boy. Eleven is the only age that is three years older, so the girl is eleven and the boy is eight.

## Page 21

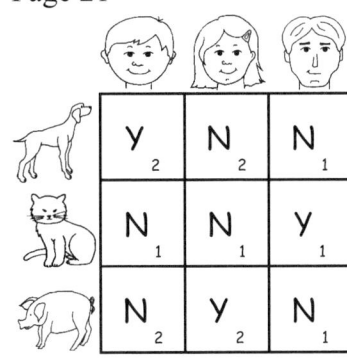

|  | dad | mom | boy |
|---|---|---|---|
| dog | Y₂ | N₂ | N₁ |
| cat | N₁ | N₁ | Y₁ |
| pig | N₂ | Y₂ | N₁ |

Clue 1 states that the dad's pet has paws and doesn't bark. Both the cat and the dog have paws, but the cat doesn't bark, so the dad's pet is the cat. Clue 2 says that the girl's pet doesn't bark, so it must be the pig. That leaves the dog as the boy's pet.

## Page 22

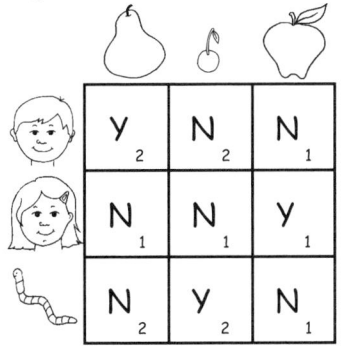

|  | pear | cherry | apple |
|---|---|---|---|
| boy | Y₂ | N₂ | N₁ |
| girl | N₁ | N₁ | Y₁ |
| worm | N₂ | Y₂ | N₁ |

Based on Clue 1, the girl's favorite fruit must be the apple since it's the only fruit that starts with an "a." Clue 2 says that the worm doesn't like the fruit that rhymes with "bear," which makes it the pear that the worm doesn't like. So the worm would like the cherry, while the boy likes the pear.

## Page 23

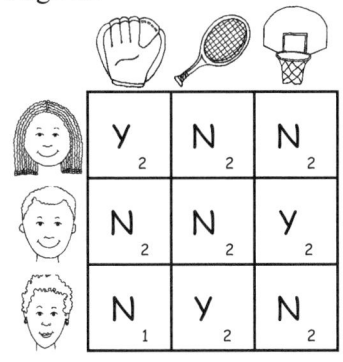

|  | glove | racket | hoop |
|---|---|---|---|
| mom | Y₂ | N₂ | N₂ |
| boy | N₂ | N₂ | Y₂ |
| girl | N₁ | Y₂ | N₂ |

Clue 1 says that mom's sport doesn't use a bat to "hit" the ball, so the mom's sport can't be baseball. Clue 2 says that the boy's sport uses the biggest ball of all three, and that would be the basketball. So that means that the mom's sport is tennis, and the girl's sport is baseball.

## Page 24

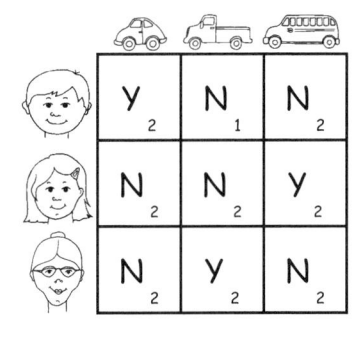

|  | car | truck | bus |
|---|---|---|---|
| boy | Y₂ | N₁ | N₂ |
| girl | N₂ | N₂ | Y₂ |
| teacher | N₂ | Y₂ | N₂ |

Clue 1 states that the boy wants to ride to school in a truck, so he now rides in either the car or the bus. Clue 2 says that the girl sits in the sixth row of seats. The only vehicle with more than four seats is the bus, so that's what the girl rides. Since the boy doesn't ride in the truck or the bus, he must ride in the car. The teacher rides in the truck.

## Page 25

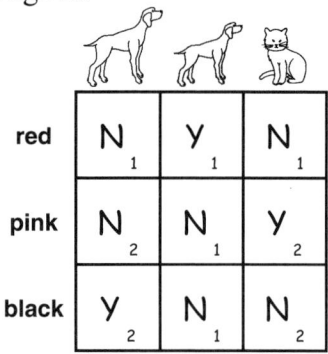

|       | 🐕 (big dog) | 🐕 (small dog) | 🐈 (cat) |
|-------|------|------|------|
| red   | N₁ | Y₁ | N₁ |
| pink  | N₂ | N₁ | Y₂ |
| black | Y₂ | N₁ | N₂ |

Based on Clue 1, the big dog and the cat like pink and black, the two colors that end in "k." That means the small dog likes red. Of the two colors left, Clue 2 says that the big dog likes the darker, which is black. That leaves the cat liking the lighter color that ends in "k," which is pink.

## Page 26

|           | Pam | Tim | Bill |
|-----------|-----|-----|------|
| dinosaur  | N₁  | N₂  | Y₂   |
| shark     | N₁  | Y₂  | N₂   |
| girl      | Y₁  | N₁  | N₁   |

In Clue 1, the girl is the only one without a tail, so the girl's name must rhyme with "ham." The girl's name is Pam. Clue 2 says that Tim swims better than Bill. Sharks swim much better than dinosaurs, so the shark's name is Tim. That leaves Bill as the dinosaur.

## Page 27

|            | pond | river | lake |
|------------|------|-------|------|
| small fish | N₁   | Y₁    | N₁   |
| medium fish| Y₂   | N₁    | N₂   |
| spotted fish| N₂  | N₁    | Y₂   |

Clue 1 says that the smallest fish has the longest home. A river is the longest of the three homes, so the smallest fish lives in the river. Clue 2 says that the spotted fish's home is not the smallest. Since a pond is smaller than a lake, the spotted fish must live in the larger of the two, the lake. The medium-sized fish lives in the pond.

## Page 28

|             | Don | Brad | Ned |
|-------------|-----|------|-----|
| boy         | Y₂  | N₂   | N₁  |
| dad         | N₂  | Y₂   | N₂  |
| grandfather | N₂  | N₂   | Y₂  |

In Clue 1, Ned is the only name that rhymes with red, so the boy's name is not Ned. In Clue 2, Brad is the only name that begins with the same sound as barn; so the dad's name is Brad, the boy's name is Don, and the grandfather's name is Ned.

## Page 29

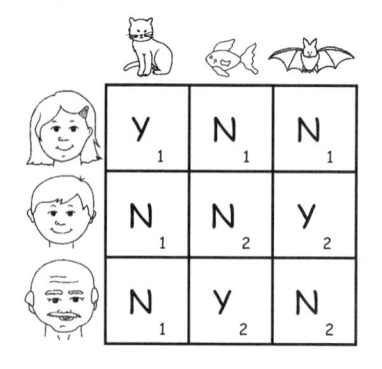

|              | cat | fish | bat |
|--------------|-----|------|-----|
| girl         | Y₁  | N₁   | N₁  |
| boy          | N₁  | N₂   | Y₂  |
| grandfather  | N₁  | Y₂   | N₂  |

In Clue 1, bat and cat both rhyme with rat, but bats can fly, so the girl's pet is the cat. In Clue 2, fish rhymes with wish, so the Grandfather's pet is the fish. The boy's pet is the bat.

## Page 30

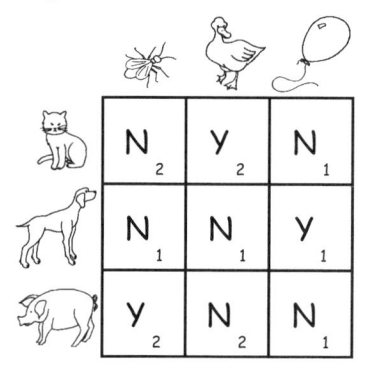

|     | fly | duck | balloon |
|-----|-----|------|---------|
| cat | N₂  | Y₂   | N₁      |
| dog | N₁  | N₁   | Y₁      |
| pig | Y₂  | N₂   | N₂      |

Clue 1 says that the cat and the pig saw things that flew away from them. Balloons don't fly, they blow or float, so the dog saw the only non-flying thing, the balloon. The cat and the pig saw either the fly or the duck. Based on Clue 2, the pig didn't see something with feathers that flies, so the pig saw the fly. That means that the cat saw the other flying thing, the duck.

Mind Benders® Level 1    Solutions

Page 31

|   | 🐱 | 🐱 | 🐱 | 🐱 |
|---|---|---|---|---|
| 👧 | N₁ | N₁ | Y₁ | N₁ |
| 👦 | N₂ | N₃ | N₁ | Y₃ |
| 👨 | Y₂ | N₂ | N₁ | N₂ |
| 👩 | N₂ | Y₃ | N₁ | N₃ |

Based on Clue 1, the girl's cat has a light tail and isn't the smallest, so it is the bigger of the two light-tailed cats. Clue 2 says that the dad's cat isn't the biggest and doesn't have a dark tail either, so it is the smaller, light-tailed cat. Clue 3 says the mom's cat is closer on the chart to the dad's cat than to the boy's cat. So mom's cat is the smaller dark-tailed cat, leaving the boy with the larger dark-tailed cat.

Page 32

|   | 🏠 | 🏠 | 🏠 | 🏠 |
|---|---|---|---|---|
| 👦 | N₂ | N₁,₂ | Y₃ | N₃ |
| 👧 | Y₂ | N₂ | N₂ | N₂ |
| 👩 | N₁ | Y₁,₂ | N₁,₂ | N₁,₂ |
| 🐕 | N₂ | N₁,₂ | N₃ | Y₃ |

Clue 1 states that the teacher's house has two windows and is next to the girl's house. Clue 2 says that the girl's house is on one end of the chart and has more than two windows. So it must be the house with three windows on the left of the chart. The teacher's house is next to the girl's, on the right. That leaves two houses: one with a black pointed roof and one with a flat roof. Clue 3 states that the boy's house has a pointed roof, so the boy's house is the one with the black roof, and the dog's is the flat-roofed house on the far right of the chart.

Page 33

|   | 👧 | 👦 | 🐱 | 🐕 |
|---|---|---|---|---|
| 🍚 | N₂ | N₃ | N₃ | Y₃ |
| 🍜 | Y₂ | N₂ | N₁ | N₁ |
| 🥣 | N₂ | N₃ | Y₃ | N₃ |
| 🥣 | N₂ | Y₃ | N₃ | N₃ |

According to Clue 1, the dog and the cat never have hot food. That leaves their choices between the two lower bowls and the top bowl, since the second bowl down is hot, with steam rising from it. Clue 2 says that the boy's bowl isn't hot, so the girl's bowl must be the hot food. Clue 3 says that the dog's bowl has the most food in it and is the same size as the cat's. The top bowl with the most food must be the dog's, and the third bowl down must be the cat's since it's the same size as the dog's. So the boy's bowl must be smallest bowl.

Page 34

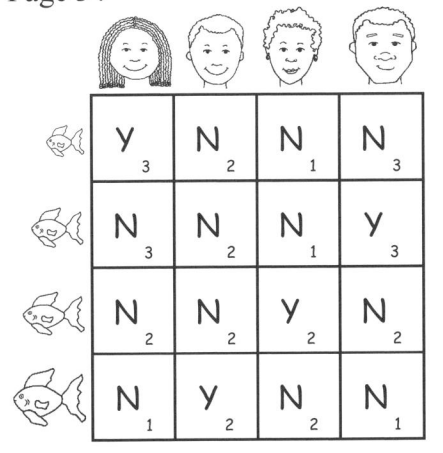

|   | 👧 | 👦 | 👦 | 👨 |
|---|---|---|---|---|
| 🐟 | Y₃ | N₂ | N₁ | N₃ |
| 🐟 | N₃ | N₂ | N₁ | Y₃ |
| 🐟 | N₂ | N₂ | Y₂ | N₂ |
| 🐟 | N₁ | Y₂ | N₂ | N₁ |

Clue 1 states that mom's fish is bigger than both the dad's and the girl's, so it has to be one of the bottom two fish. This means that neither the girl nor the dad could have the largest fish. Since Clue 2 says the boy's fish is bigger than mom's, it is the largest fish. That leaves the fish above it as the mom's. Clue 3 states that the dad's fish is not the smallest. That makes the smallest fish the girl's and the second smallest fish the dad's.

Page 35

|   | 1 | 3 | 4 | 6 |
|---|---|---|---|---|
| 👧 | Y₂ | N₁ | N₁ | N₂ |
| 👦 | N₂ | N₁ | N₁ | Y₂ |
| 👩 | N₁ | N₃ | Y₃ | N₁ |
| 👨 | N₁ | Y₃ | N₃ | N₁ |

Based on Clue 1, the parents caught three or four fish, not the fewest (1) and not the most (6). This also means, then, that neither the daughter nor the son caught three or four fish. Clue 2 says that the daughter caught fewer fish than her brother. So she caught the fewest, and the brother caught the largest number of fish. Clue 3 says that the mother caught more fish than the father. That means the mother caught four and the father caught three.

Page 36

|   | 1st | 2nd | 3rd | 4th |
|---|---|---|---|---|
| cat | N₂ | N₁ | Y₂ | N₁ |
| dog | N₁ | Y₂ | N₁ | N₂ |
| cat | Y₂ | N₁ | N₂ | N₁ |
| dog | N₁ | N₂ | N₁ | Y₂ |

Clue 1 states that a cat was first and third in the running race. So, neither cat was second or fourth, and no dog was first or third. Clue 2 says that the little dog finished before both the little cat and the big dog. That means the little dog was second, the little cat was third, and the big dog was fourth. So the big cat was first and won the race.

Page 37

|   | 6 | 7 | 8 | 9 |
|---|---|---|---|---|
| shark | Y₂ | N₁ | N₁ | N₂ |
| cat | N₁ | N₃ | Y₃ | N₁ |
| dog | N₁ | Y₃ | N₃ | N₁ |
| duck | N₂ | N₁ | N₁ | Y₂ |

Using Clue 1, the two creatures who have legs adding up to eight, the dog and the cat, aren't the youngest or the oldest, so one would be seven and one would be eight years old. This also means that neither the shark nor the duck could be seven or eight years old, instead they are either six or nine. Clue 2 states that the oldest doesn't have fins, so it's not the shark, which leaves the nine-year-old duck. The youngest, then, is the shark at six years. Clue 3 states that the dog was at the cat's seventh birthday party last year, so the cat is now eight. That makes the dog seven years old.

Page 38

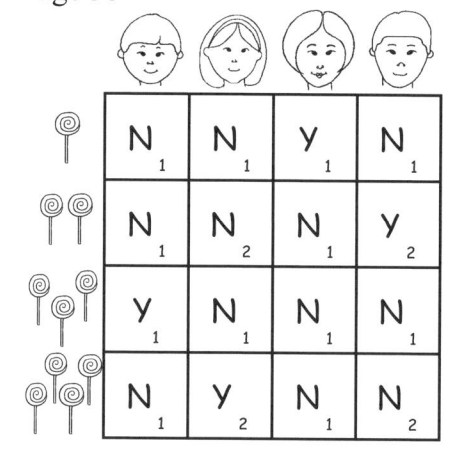

|   | boy | girl | mom | dad |
|---|---|---|---|---|
| 1 | N₁ | N₁ | Y₁ | N₁ |
| 2 | N₁ | N₂ | N₁ | Y₂ |
| 3 | Y₁ | N₁ | N₁ | N₁ |
| 4 | N₁ | Y₂ | N₁ | N₂ |

Based on Clue 1, the mom bought only one sucker, the fewest of all. The boy bought two more than the mom, so he bought three. Clue 2 says that the father bought fewer suckers than the boy, which leaves the father buying two suckers, which is more than one. The girl bought four suckers.

Page 39

|        | 👧 | 👦 | 👧 | 👦 |
|--------|---|---|---|---|
| Nancy  | Y₁ | N₁ | N₁ | N₁ |
| Bill   | N₁ | N₁ | N₁ | Y₁ |
| Sandy  | N₁ | N₁ | Y₁ | N₁ |
| Jack   | N₁ | Y₁ | N₁ | N₁ |

The solution is based on the only clue given, the heights of the children across the top of the chart, and whether they're a boy or girl. The tall boy and girl are the same height, and the shorter boy and girl are the same height. Clue 1 states that Bill is taller than Jack and Nancy. That means Bill is the taller of the two boys and on the far right of the chart. Jack is the shorter boy. If Bill is taller than Nancy, it means that Sandy is his same height. So Nancy is the smaller girl on the far left of the chart.

Page 40

|     | dog | cat | bat | rat |
|-----|-----|-----|-----|-----|
| 👧  | N₁ | Y₃ | N₃ | N₂ |
| 👦  | N₁ | N₂ | N₂ | Y₂ |
| 👨  | Y₁ | N₁ | N₁ | N₁ |
| 👩  | N₁ | N₃ | Y₃ | N₂ |

Clue 1 states that the name of dad's pet doesn't rhyme with the name of anyone else's pet. The only pet name that doesn't rhyme with the others is dog, so that's the dad's pet. Clue 2 says that the girl's pet's name and the mom's pet's name both rhyme with rat. That means neither the girl nor the mom has a rat, so their pets are the cat or the bat. Thus the boy has the rat. Based on Clue 3, the mom's pet isn't the cat, so it must be the bat. That means the cat is the girl's pet.

Page 41

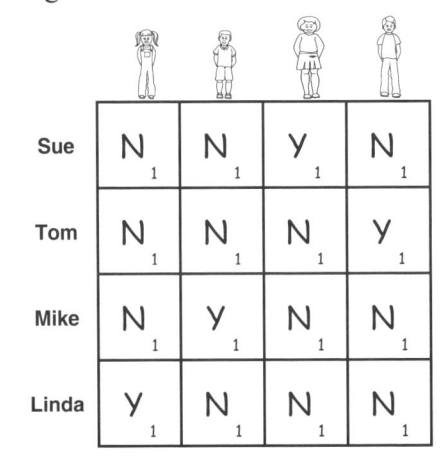

|       | 👧 | 👦 | 👧 | 👦 |
|-------|---|---|---|---|
| Sue   | N₁ | N₁ | Y₁ | N₁ |
| Tom   | N₁ | N₁ | N₁ | Y₁ |
| Mike  | N₁ | Y₁ | N₁ | N₁ |
| Linda | Y₁ | N₁ | N₁ | N₁ |

This puzzle has a tall boy and girl, and a short boy and girl. The only clue states that Tom is taller than Linda. That means that Linda is the shorter girl and Sue is the taller girl. Also, Tom is taller than the other boy, whose name must be Mike.

Page 42

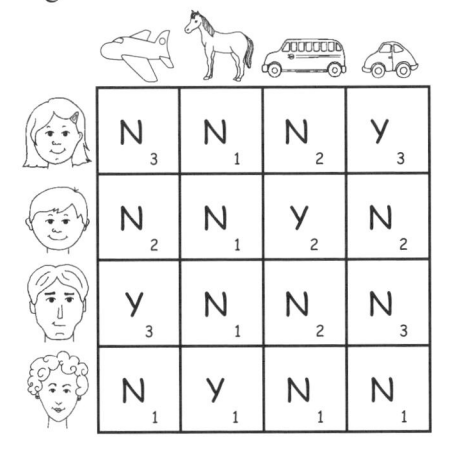

|     | ✈ | 🐴 | 🚌 | 🚗 |
|-----|---|---|---|---|
| 👩  | N₃ | N₁ | N₂ | Y₃ |
| 👦  | N₂ | N₁ | Y₂ | N₂ |
| 👨  | Y₃ | N₁ | N₂ | N₃ |
| 👧  | N₁ | Y₁ | N₁ | N₁ |

Clue 1 states that the woman's hair was rained on her whole trip, so she was riding the horse. Clue 2 states that the boy could look out sixteen windows, so he rode the bus (the two front windows have no seats). Clue 3 says that the girl's purse was next to her, and her suitcase was in the trunk. The vehicle with a trunk is the car, which is what the girl rode in. That leaves the man riding on the plane.

# Page 43

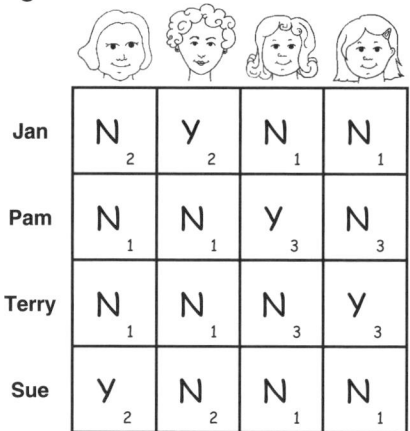

|  | 🙂 | 🙂 | 🙂 | 🙂 |
|---|---|---|---|---|
| Jan | N₂ | Y₂ | N₁ | N₁ |
| Pam | N₁ | N₁ | Y₃ | N₃ |
| Terry | N₁ | N₁ | N₃ | Y₃ |
| Sue | Y₂ | N₂ | N₁ | N₁ |

In Clue 1, if Jan drives Pam and Terry to their soccer game, then Jan must be one of the women, and Pam and Terry are the children. So Sue must be the other adult. According to Clue 2, if Sue used to drive Jan to school, then Sue is older than Jan. So Sue is the grandmother and Jan is the mother. Based on Clue 3, Terry is the girl with straight hair, so Pam has the curly hair.